"The Demons of War ɛ

A Personal Story of Prolonged PTSD

—A.W. Schade, USMC 1965/69

Fifty years have passed since my deployment as a combat Marine to Vietnam. However, only several years since I acknowledged my inability to continue suppressing the demons alone. Like many veterans, the "Demons" have haunted me through nightmares, altered personas, and hidden fears.

Even as many veterans manage the demons' onslaught successfully, millions survive in destitution, needless solitude and social disconnection. Scores consider themselves cowards, should they concede to the demons' hold. Countless live in denial and loneliness, protecting their warrior's pride. The most vulnerable— tormented by guilt and feeling forever alone — too often choose to "end" their lives.

www.awschade.com   awschade@gmail.com

As friends and family gather to celebrate another joyful holiday, I am often disheartened, reminded by vivid memories of lost friendships and battlefield carnage that erratically seeps from a vulnerable partition of my mind. The cerebral hiding place I concocted, decades before, as a mechanism to survive in society. I unwittingly clutch at a profound loneliness as I avoid searching for memories of my youthful years. If I dare to gaze into my past, I must transcend a cloak of darkness weaved to restrain the demons from so many years before.

My pledge to God, Country, and Marine Corps was more than forty years ago. As a young, unproven warrior, I consented to the ancient rules of war. At eighteen, like many others, I was immersed in the ageless stench of death and carnage, in the mountains and jungles of Vietnam. However, my journey began much earlier, on a sixty-mile bus ride with other nervous teenagers, to New York City's legendary Induction Center at 39 White Hall Street.

We went through lines of examinations and stood around for hours, recognizing one another's bare asses before we could learn each other's names. We did not realize so many of us would remain together in squads and fire teams, building deep-seeded bonds of friendships along our journey. Our initial 'shock' indoctrination began immediately at Parris

Page 1

Island; intimidating Drill Instructors scrambled our disoriented butts off the bus, organized us into a semblance of a formation, and herded us to the barracks for a night of hell!

Anxiety, second-guessing our decision to join, and apprehension was our welcoming. Following what we thought would be sleep (but was actually a nap), we awoke in awe to explosive clamor, as the DIs banged on tin garbage can lids next to our bunks, yelling 'get up you maggots.' Even the largest recruits trembled.

We remained maggots for the next few weeks and began intense physical and mental training, slowly recognizing the importance of "the team" instead of "the individual." In less than sixteen weeks we were proud United States Marines. It was a short celebration though, as we loaded our gear and headed, in order, to Camp Lejeune, Camp Pendleton, Okinawa and then the Philippines, where we continued to enhance our stealth and killing skills, before executing these talents on the already blood-soaked fields of Vietnam.

We argued and fought amongst ourselves as brothers often do. Still, we never lost sight of the bonds we shared: We were United States Marines with an indisputable commitment to "always cover each other's back." Crammed into the bowels of Navy Carrier Ships, we slept in hammocks with no more than three inches from your brother's butt above you. The sailors laughed as these self-proclaimed "bad-ass Marines" transformed into the wimpy "Helmet Brigade." We vomited into our skull buckets for days on our way to Okinawa, where we would engage in counter guerrilla warfare training. Aware that we were going to Vietnam, we partied hard in every port. The first of our battles were slug fests in distant bar-room brawls.

Conversely, our minds were opened to the poverty and living conditions of these famous islands in the Pacific. Their reputations preceded them, but stories about war with Japan—John Wayne movies—were not what we found. Instead, we found overpopulated, dirty cities; we were barraged constantly by poor children seeking any morsel of food. In the fields, families lived in thatched huts with no electricity or sanitary conditions. While training I experienced the horror of being chased by a two-ton water

www.awschade.com   awschade@gmail.com

buffalo (with only blanks in my rifle). Moments before, this same beast was led around by a ring through its nose by a ten-year old boy. Worse than the chasing was hearing the laughter of brother Marines watching me run at full speed, trying to find something to climb. In a tree, I felt as though I was losing the "macho" in Marine, and we were still thousands of miles from Vietnam.

In confidence, we spoke as brothers about our fears, hardships growing-up, family, girlfriends, times of humiliation, prejudice, and what we planned to do in our lifetime once our tour of duty in Vietnam was over. We knew each other's thoughts and spoke as though we would all return home alive, never considering the thought of death or defeat. We had not learned that lesson, yet. Moreover, we dreamed of going home as respected American warriors who defended democracy in a remote foreign land, standing proud, feeling a sense of accomplishment, and experiencing life, as none of our friends at home would understand. Our country had called and we answered.

We transferred to a converted WWII aircraft carrier that carried helicopters and Marines instead of jet planes. We were to traverse the coast of Vietnam and deploy by helicopter into combat zones from the Demilitarized Zone, the imaginary line separating North and South Vietnam, to the provinces and cities of Chu Lai and Da Nang. Then further south, to the outer fringes of Vietnam's largest city, which was, at that time, Saigon.

Within sight of land, we heard the roar of artillery, mortars and the familiar crackling of small-arms fire. These were sounds we were accustomed to because of months of preparing ourselves for battle. However, for the first time, we understood the sounds were not from playing war games. Someone was likely dead. Anxiety, adrenaline highs, and fear of the unknown swirled within my mind.

Was I prepared? Could I kill another man? Would another man kill me? From that point forward, death was part of my life. We would eventually load into helicopters, descending into confrontations ambivalent, yet assured we were young, invincible warriors. We were convinced the South

Vietnamese people needed us; many of them did. Thus, our mission was simple: save the innocent and banish the enemy to Hell!

The first time we touched down on Vietnam soil, we mechanically spread out in combat formation. Immediately, everything I was taught to watch out for rushed through my mind: "Was the enemy around us?" "Was I standing near an enemy grenade trap, or stepping toward a punji pit filled with sharpened bamboo spikes?" Seeing our company walking through the low brush gave me comfort, until an unexpected explosion deafened our senses. We immediately hit the ground and went into combat mode, establishing our zones of fire. There was nothing to think about except engaging the enemy. We were ready for battle.

We waited, but heard no gunfire or rockets exploding, only a few Marines speaking several hundred feet away. One yelled, "I can't F'N" believe it!" We learned our first meeting with death was due to one of our brother's grenade pins not being secured; we assumed it was pulled out by the underbrush. Regardless, he was dead. Staring at his lifeless body, I felt the loss of youthful innocence gush away.

One engagement began with us being plunged into chaos from helicopters hovering a few feet off the ground. We anxiously leapt—some fell—into the midst of an already heated battle. The enemy sprung a deadly assault upon us. I became engrossed in the shock, fear, and adrenaline rush of battle. It was surreal! It was also not the time to ponder the killing of another human being, recall the rationale behind the ethics of war, or become absorbed in the horror of men slaughtering each other. Thoughts of war's demons certainly were not on my mind.

When the killing ceased and the enemy withdrew, I remained motionless, exhausted from the fighting. With only a moment to think about what had just occurred, the shock, hate, and anger were buried under the gratitude of being alive. I had to find out which brothers did or did not survive, and as I turned to view the combat zone, I witnessed the reality of war: dreams, friendships, and future plans vanished. We knelt beside our brothers, some dead, many wounded, and others screaming in pain. A few lay there dying silently.

Page 4

As I moved about the carnage, I noticed a lifeless body, face down, and twisted abnormally in jungle debris. I pulled him gently from the tangled lair, unaware of the warrior I had found. Masked in blood and shattered bones, I was overwhelmed with disgust and a primal obsession for revenge as I realized the warrior was my mentor, hero, and friend.

My voice fragmented, I spoke at him as if he were alive: "Gunny, you can't be dead! Son-of-a-bitch, you fought in WWII and Korea, how can you die in this God for-shaken country! Get up Marine!" Tears seeped down my face; I whispered that he would not be forgotten. I placed him gently in a body bag, slowly pulling the zipper closed over his face, engulfing him in darkness.

Navy Corpsmen—our extraordinary brothers—worked frantically to salvage traumatized bodies. We did our best to ease the pain of the wounded as they prayed to God Almighty. "With all my heart I love you, man," I told each friend I encountered. However, some never heard the words I said, unless they were listening from Heaven. I was unaware of the survivor's guilt brewing deep inside me.

In two or three weeks our mission was completed; we flew by helicopter from the jungle to the safety of the ship. None of us rested, instead remembering faces and staring at the empty bunks of the friends who were not there. I prayed for the sun to rise slowly, in order to delay the forthcoming ceremony for the dead.

Early the next morning, we stood in a military formation on the aircraft carrier's deck. I temporarily suppressed my emotions as I stared upon the dead. Rows of military caskets, identical in design, with an American flag meticulously draped over the top, made it impossible to distinguish which crates encased my closest friends. As taps played, tears descended. For the first time I understood, that in war, you never have a chance to say goodbye. I pledged silently to each of my friends that they would never be forgotten: A solemn promise I regretfully only kept through years of nightmares or hallucinations.

Combat is vicious; rest is brief; destroying the enemy was our mission. We fought our skillful foes in many battles, until they or we were dead,

www.awschade.com   awschade@gmail.com

wounded, or overwhelmed. Engaging enemy troops was horrific in both jungles and villages. We had to either accept or build psychological boundaries around the terror.

Nonexistent were the lines of demarcation; we constantly struggled to identify which Vietnamese was a friend and which was a foe. The tormenting acknowledgement that a woman or child might be an enemy combatant had to be confronted; it was often an overwhelming decision to make.

I was not aware of the change in my demeanor. In time, I merely assumed I had adjusted emotionally to contend with the atrocities and finality of war. I acquired stamina, could endure the stench of death, eliminate enemy combatants with little or no remorse, suppress memories of fallen companions, and avoid forming new, deep-rooted friendships. I struggled to accept the feasibility of a loving Lord. I never detected the nameless demons embedding themselves inside of me.

At the end of my tour, I packed minimal gear and left the jungle battlefields of Vietnam for America, never turning to bid farewell or ever wanting to smell the pungent stench of death and fear again. Within seventy-two hours, I was on the street I left fourteen months prior, a street untouched by war, poverty, genocide, hunger, or fear.

I was home. I was alone. Aged well beyond my chronological years of nine-teen, I was psychologically and emotionally confused. I was expected to transform from a slayer back into a (so-called) civilized man.

Except for family members and several high-school friends, returning home from Vietnam was demeaning for most of us. There were no bands or cheers of appreciation or feelings of accomplishment. Instead, we were shunned and ridiculed for fighting in a war that our government assured us was crucial and for an honorable cause. I soon found that family, friends, and co-workers could never truly understand the events that transformed me in those fourteen months.

I changed from a teenage boy to a battle hardened man. I was not able to engage in trivial conversations or take part in the adolescent games many of my friends still played. For them, life did not change and "struggle" was a job or the "unbearable" pressure of college they had to endure. It did not take me long to realize that they would never understand; there is no comparison between homework and carrying a dead companion in a black zipped bag.

The media played their biased games by criticizing the military, never illuminating the thousands of Vietnamese saved from mass execution, rape, torture, or other atrocities of a brutal northern regime. They never showed the stories of American "heroes" who gave their lives, bodies, and minds to save innocent people caught in the clutches of a "controversial" war. For years, my transition back to society was uncertain. I struggled against unknown demons and perplexing social fears. I abandoned searching for surviving comrades or ever engaging in conversations of Vietnam.

Worse, I fought alone to manage the recurring nightmares, which I tried to block away in a chamber of my mind labeled; "Do not open, horrors, chaos and lost friends from Vietnam." However, suppressing dark memories is almost impossible. Random sounds, smells, or even words unleash nightmares, depression, anxiety and the seepage's of bitterness I alluded to before. I still fight to keep these emotions locked away inside me.

Today, my youth has long since passed and middle age is drifting progressively behind me. Still, unwelcome metaphors and echoes of lost souls seep through the decomposing barriers fabricated in my mind. Vivid memories of old friends, death, guilt, and anger sporadically persevere. There may be no end, resolution, or limitations to the demons' voices. They began as whispers and intensified—over decades—in my mind.

"Help me buddy!" I still hear them scream, as nightmares jolt me from my slumber. I wake and shout, "I'm here! I'm here my friend," and envision their ghostly, blood-soaked bodies. I often wonder if more Marines would be alive if I had fought more fiercely. "I had to kill!" I remind myself; as visions of shattered friends, and foes hauntingly reappear at inappropriate times.

www.awschade.com   awschade@gmail.com

Guilt consumes my consciousness as I recall the mayhem of war, and what we had to do to survive. As well I question: Why did I survive and not them? Most horrible, however, is the conflicting torment I feel when I acknowledge that I am thankful it was others instead of me.

Regardless of which war a person fought, I am sure many of their memories are similar to mine, as many of mine are to theirs. I never recognized the persistence of the demons, nor realized how quickly they matured deep within my soul. Disguised and deep-rooted, the demons cause anxiety, loneliness, depression, alcohol abuse, nightmares, and suicidal thoughts; traits that haunt many warriors for a lifetime. For thirty-five years, I would not admit these demons were inside me, and believed seeking medical assistance for what was going on in my mind, was a weakness in a man.

It was not until the first Gulf War began in 1990, that I sensed the demons were again bursting from within. No matter how hard I tried to avoid them, I could not escape the vivid images and news coverage of every aspect of the war. Eventually, the bodies and faces in the media were not strangers anymore; they were the faces of my brothers from a much older and forgotten war. Encouraged by peers and several family members, I finally sought assistance from VA doctors, who immediately diagnosed me with PTSD and began an ongoing treatment program.

During my third or fourth group therapy session at the VA, the psychiatrist leading the meeting persuaded me to speak about myself, starting with my overall thoughts of my tour in Vietnam, but then focusing on what I accomplished instead of what I lost. After a long hesitation, I told them the greatest accomplishment in Vietnam was the hundreds of people our teams personally saved from rape, torture, or savage death.

We did not give a damn about the politicians and college students arguing back home, or running off to Canada to avoid the draft. We were enlisted Marines, on the front lines, protecting innocent people caught up in a horrific war.

My most positive moment, I continued, was when I lifted a three-year-old girl from the rubble that separated her from her parents, who were

www.awschade.com   awschade@gmail.com

slaughtered by the Viet Cong for giving us rice the day before. Though traumatized and trembling in fear, she reached up to me, and I cradled her gently in my arms and made her smile for only a moment. I handed her to one of our extraordinary corpsman, and continued to seek out the enemy who committed these atrocious murders. It was then I understood why I was in Vietnam.

However, as with everything I masked in my subconscious, I obscured that moment of compassion for decades until this small therapy group encouraged me to glance back and look for positive events buried within the worst of my war memories.

Regarding my post-war years, the doctor asked me to focus on my career, an area where he knew I had some success. I explained that when I left the Marines after four years, I was youthful and confident in myself. I had no clue what depression and anxiety were, and I thought the nightmares were personal and temporary. I was determined to look forward, and in no way backwards to the war. Unfortunately, today I realize that while constantly looking forward helped me avoid chaotic memories of war, it also cloaked the memories of my formative younger years, and positive events throughout my life.

I never relished talking about myself, and thought it would be a good time to stop. However, the group asked me to continue. As peers, they knew I needed to feel a purpose, and not think my life was a second-rate existence. I was reluctant; as I looked around the room and knew many of the Vets succumbed to PTSD early in life and did not fare as well as I did. I felt I was about to sound like a wimp, or worse, a self-centered ass.

Awkwardly, I began to tell them - with many gaps - about my career after Vietnam. My first recollection was one they all understood. I went through eleven or twelve jobs feeling totally out of place. Watching sales managers gather their teams, and with fanatical enthusiasm tell us how great we were, and together we would attain the highest sales revenue, whipping all other regions. To me, compared to combat in the jungles of Vietnam, this was a game.

www.awschade.com   awschade@gmail.com

Feeling extremely frustrated within the environment of civilian life, I was ready to head back to the military. However, before reenlistment happened, I got married to my current wife of 40 plus years, who will be the first to tell you living with a type-A personality with PTSD is often a living hell, especially since she had no idea what I was battling. But, neither did I. Like millions of warriors before me, I never spoke to anyone about the war, or the nightmares that abruptly woke me, soaked in sweat and tears.

I decided not to reenlist and pursued a career in business. After numerous jobs, I finally landed a position with a bank repossessing cars - a small-scale adrenalin rush, at times. Within five years, I worked my way up to branch manager.

Bored, of my repetitive tasks in banking, I accepted an offer from a very large computer company to join as a collection administrator. Though it seemed as if it was starting over, I was promoted into management within a year. Focusing on new business challenges aided me in keeping the demons at bay. Subsequent promotions followed.

Within roughly eight years, I was selected to attend Syracuse University to attain a degree in Management - paid by the company at full salary. I continued to accept challenging positions in finance, marketing, business development, sales and world travel.

At first, traveling to other countries was great, but after the second or third twenty-one-hour flight to Bangkok or Singapore, it got old quick. I began to realize boredom and repetition were major catalysts for my emotional setbacks; having too much time to think was a recipe for falling hard into the bowels of PTSD.

As years passed, anger, frustrations, mood swings, and depression were common events affecting me, my family and career. I stopped moving forward, and spent more time battling the memories of the past. It was at that time I understood the demons never leave; they simply wait for a sliver of weakness to overwhelm you.

www.awschade.com   awschade@gmail.com

Consequently, these conditions, as well as heightened road-rage, quick to anger, and sometimes not able to carry on an articulate conversation, I unenthusiastically retired early from my very well-paying job. This, of course, decreased my income significantly, and opened new crevices in my rapidly deteriorating armor. The demons seized a stronghold; they are persistent.

I have still not won the battle against the demons, but, with the help of therapy, outside physical activities, medications and writing; I look ahead again. The demons continue to haunt me with nightmares, depression, memory loss, anxiety and the need for solitude.

Although I am not able to sit down with a vet and talk about war, I have taken on a cause through writing stories, to reach out to young and senior veterans to help break the stigma of PTSD, by seeking reinforcement. It took me, with present-day support from younger vets at the Journal of Military Experience [http://militaryexperience.org], over the course of six years to finalize this story. I mention this so others can move forward in his or her life; by knowing what I and others know now.

I wish someone cited the following recommendations to me earlier in my life; although being young and macho I probably would not have listened. However, here are a few suggestions from one old warrior, to those of all ages:

- Break through the stigma of PTSD and get medical assistance - PTSD is real!
- Unless you are in a high-risk job, you will probably not experience the adrenaline rush and finality of your decisions as you did in combat. For me, I lived by playing business games - never finding the ultimate adrenaline rush again. It is a void within me, I think about often.
- The longer you wait for treatment, the harder it will be to handle the demons. They do not go away and can lay dormant in your soul for decades.
- Understand that it is never too late in your life to begin looking forward and achieving new objectives.
- If you do not want to speak about PTSD with your family or friends, then hand them a brochure from the VA that explains what to look

www.awschade.com   awschade@gmail.com

for, and why you need their support. You do not have to go into detail about the tragedies of war, but without your loved ones' understanding of your internal battle, your thoughts can lead to divorce, loss of family relationship, or suicide – a terrible waste of a hero.

- Silence and solitude is not the answer! If you have PTSD you may not be able to beat it alone.
- If you are concerned about your military or civilian job, seek help from peer resources. They have experienced what you have been through, and will help keep you living in the present, instead of the past.
- Or contact a person in a peer support group anonymously. They will not know you, but will talk for as long as you wish.
- You cannot explain the horrors of war to someone that has not experienced it, except maybe a PTSD psychologist.
- Get up off your ass and take a serious look into yourself! Accept the fact that if you have continuous nightmares, flashbacks, depression, bursts of anger, anxiety, or thoughts of suicide, you have PTSD. If so, talk to someone who can help.
- There is also financial assistance through the VA, which may help you avoid living a life of destitution.

Finally, let your ego and macho image go. There are many individuals and groups today wanting to help you. If you do not seek help, you may find yourself alone and bitter for a lifetime. The demons are not going away, but with help, you can learn to fight them and win one battle at a time. Please contact the resources below!

Semper Fi!

[AW Schade; a Marine, Vietnam 1966/67, retired corporate executive and author of the award-winning book, *Looking for God within the Kingdom of Religious Confusion.* A captivating, comparative, and enlightening tale that seeks to comprehend the doctrines and discord between and within Judaism, Christianity, Islam, and Secularism. What the seeker discovers, transforms his life forever!]

www.awschade.com   awschade@gmail.com

Not Alone

Not Alone

A Veterans discovery in a 'peer-to-peer' support group

AW Schade
USMC 1965/69

www.awschade.com   awschade@gmail.com

Not Alone

—A.W. Schade, USMC 1965/69

Just before I entered the small meeting room for my fourth group therapy session at the VA, my psychiatrist motioned me to his office. This was not unusual. He often spoke to me before my session when his schedule permitted, and I appreciated those brief moments. After several months of one-on-one therapy sessions, I had gained a level of trust with him that I have shared with very few people since the atrocities of war in Vietnam.

But this time I sensed I was about to receive a suggestion I may not be ready for. In his normal reassuring demeanor he shook my hand and asked me to sit down. I immediately felt my anxiety build, not from fear, but anticipation "Art," he said, "it is time for you to move to the next level of therapy."

"And what is that?" I asked, as if I did not know.

During the previous group sessions, I had listened to other veterans' stories and participated in several meaningful conversations, but I had not yet told my own story. "It is time for you to begin disclosing the agony lodged within you with the rest of the group," he told me.

He rose from his chair, patted me on my shoulder and left his office, leaving me to sit in silence for the next few minutes to absorb the full meaning of what he asked me to do.

I knew it would be okay with him if I delayed discussing my personal struggles for another session. At fifty-eight years old talking about my nightmares, panic attacks and depression with a fine psychiatrist doing his best to help me cope, was not the same as engaging others who had experienced the emotional conflicts of combat. I would wait to see how the session was progressing before making my decision.

www.awschade.com   awschade@gmail.com

I looked at my watch and realized I was going to be a few minutes late for our group session. My anxiety level rose. Ever since my experiences in combat, I have been obsessed with being on time. I demanded it of myself, and expected it from family, friends, and even employees throughout my corporate career. I started every meeting on time and locked the meeting room door for those who consistently showed up late. It was only years later, here in these small gatherings with other veterans, that I understood my fixation on timeliness. The connection was rather simple: in combat not being in your firing position, or flanking the enemy on time, could cause death.

I entered the windowless classroom just as our group leader was closing the door. I knew one of the guys already seated would make a comment, and he did not disappoint. "Hey Mr. timeliness," he said, "you are late!" We all laughed, as I sat down in the open chair in the semi-circle reserved for the "late ass."

Looking around the room at my fellow veterans, who all served in Vietnam, I remembered my reluctance four weeks earlier to join group therapy. But my psychiatrist had convinced me that the proper group may help to heal the anxiety, depression and guilt I suppressed in tormented memories. I told him I would try it the following week, and for the next several days I regretted making that commitment. For thirty-five years I had not spoken to anyone about the war and the inhumanities we encountered, or sought out any of my Marine Corps buddies who had made that journey through Hell with me.

I imagined guys sitting in a room telling 'Rambo' type war stories. Old men, telling each other what they could have been, how life screwed them, or arguing that their tour of duty was worse than the others. And I had no desire to listen to someone who had a desk job and was safe throughout his tour telling stories of his war exploits. Nothing against those not in the line of fire, everyone had an important job to do, but I had low expectations that the sessions would help me.

But who was I to know what was best. The VA doctors did a very good job of blending members of our group together. All but one of the eight group were in combat in Vietnam. A few lived with physical combat disabilities, and one spent decades in psychiatric care.

www.awschade.com   awschade@gmail.com

The one veteran that did not participate in combat was respectful, did not try to fit in by telling bogus war stories, and spoke very little. It was not until some gentle probing by the group leader, a compassionate sociologist, that he told us about his experiences, which he felt weren't as significant as ours. Speaking softly he said one of his primary duties was unloading hundreds of body bags a week off helicopters, all holding the remains of kids his age. Later he helped load the coffins on airplanes for the journey home for those unappreciated heroes.

As I listened, my eyes filled with tears and I saw images of the dead friends I zipped into the same type bags he mentioned. I wondered if he handled any of my friends, and treated the standard black bags with honor. I also thought about his desolation, and wanted to ask him how he felt when he lifted a bag and realized it was unstable, filled with a warrior's body parts rolling about inside, instead of an intact body. But I knew my questions could wait until he was ready to discuss them. That was an unmentioned condition of group therapy. As he continued, I realized for the first time that the agony and haunting memories of war are not felt only by those in battle.

It was never easy to cry, or to witness a group of older men crying, especially knowing the emotional pain that had been bound within them for decades. But we respected each other and our weekly sessions helped us to share our common frustrations, guilt and anger, and happier moments as well.

We did not resolve all of our problems, nor did we expect to, but for that hour I knew that others "had my back." I realized I had been unconsciously searching for that since I left active duty. It was a special bond I shared with fellow Marines, close friends or even those I disliked, that was ingrained in us during Marine Corps training, and reinforced time and again in the jungles of Vietnam.

Of course, there have been people since the war that I have considered friends. But only a rare few met my subconscious criteria of someone who would die for me, with me confident that I would do the same for him. This expectation has had a direct effect on my feelings of loneliness, but my criteria have not changed, nor do I expect they will.

Group therapy is not the cure-all for the aftermath of trauma. But it helped me understand myself, my life's choices and the rational for the decisions I made, and continue to make. We were there to help each other fight the common demons of Post-Traumatic Stress Disorder, deeply embedded within us. Understanding this, we set aside our differences and focused on the current battle we had in common.

During that fourth session it was my turn. The group leader asked me if I would like to speak about my demons, starting with my overall thoughts of my tour in Vietnam, and focusing on what I accomplished, instead of what I lost. I knew my time had come to discuss my feelings with the group. After a long hesitation, I told them my greatest accomplishment in Vietnam was the hundreds of people our teams personally saved from rape, torture, or savage death.

I did not believe the frustration I held inside me would flow so easily, and I continued in a somewhat aggressive manner. "We did not give a damn about the politicians and college students arguing back home, or running off to Canada to avoid the draft," I said. "We were enlisted Marines, on the front lines, protecting innocent people caught up in a horrific war. We lost the war because we were not given the opportunity to win it. It was a political and social farce that resulted in us being branded 'baby killers' and losers!" It was a brief statement, but we would come back to it for several sessions to discuss the agony and humiliation we all shared.

After my emotional start, and aware this topic would not be resolved during that session, the group leader allowed me to sit there silently and compose myself. A few moments later, he asked me to speak about my most positive moment, if there is such a thing in combat.

"My most positive moment," I continued, "was when I lifted a three-year-old girl from the rubble that separated her from her parents, who had been slaughtered the night before by the Viet Cong for giving us rice. Though traumatized and trembling in fear, she reached up to me. I knelt beside her and cradled her gently in my arms. It might be my aging imagination, but I thought for sure for a brief moment I made her smile. I handed her to one of our extraordinary corpsmen, and continued to seek out the enemy who committed these atrocious murders. It was then that I understood why I was in Vietnam."

I had obscured that moment of compassion for decades until this small therapy group encouraged me to glance back and look for positive events tangled within my worst memories of war. I remember several group members telling me, "You have to keep that memory proudly in your heart, when the worst memories overtake you."

The group leader asked me to talk about my post-war years, an area where he knew I had some success. I told them that when I left the Marines after four years, I was youthful and confident in myself. I had no clue what depression and anxiety were, and I thought the nightmares were personal and temporary. I was determined to look forward, not backwards to the war. Unfortunately, today I realize that while constantly looking forward helped me avoid chaotic memories of war, it also cloaked the memories of my formative younger years, and positive events throughout my life.

I have never relished talking about myself, and wanted to stop, but the group asked me to continue. As peers, they knew I needed to feel a purpose, and not think my life was a second-rate existence. I was reluctant. I knew many of the vets in the room had succumbed to PTSD early in life and did not fare as well as I did. I felt I was about to sound like a wimp, or worse, a self-centered ass.

Awkwardly, I began to tell them about my career after Vietnam. My first recollection was one they all understood. I went through eleven or twelve jobs feeling totally out of place. Sales managers gathered their teams, and with fanatical enthusiasm told us how great we were, and that together we would attain the highest sales, whipping all other regions. To me, compared to combat in the jungles of Vietnam, this was a game.

Feeling extremely frustrated within the environment of civilian life, I was ready to head back to the military. Instead I got married to my current wife of 42 years, who will tell you that living with a type-A personality with PTSD is often a living hell, especially since she had no idea what I was battling. But, neither did I. Like millions of warriors before me, I never spoke to anyone about the war, or the nightmares that abruptly woke me, soaked in sweat and tears.

I pursued a career in business, and excelled. Initially, traveling to other countries was great, but twenty-one hour flights to Bangkok or

Singapore got old quick. The boredom and repetition were major catalysts for my emotional setbacks; having too much time to think was a recipe for falling hard into the bowels of PTSD. Anger, frustrations, mood swings, and depression were common. I had stopped moving forward, and spent more time battling the memories of the past. It was then that I understood the demons never leave; they simply wait for a sliver of weakness to overwhelm you. They are persistent.

I had dealt with this on my own until the First Gulf War in 1990, when everywhere I turned I saw vivid pictures of death, battles and impoverished families. I couldn't escape the memories of Vietnam. I still did not accept I had PTSD, but my brother-in-law, who had been treated for it for years, was persistent and talked me into getting a quick check up. Three psychiatrists later, I was diagnosed with PTSD and for the first time understood about the demons I had been fighting alone for forty years.

The road would be a long one, and my demons would continue to haunt me with nightmares, depression, memory loss, anxiety and the need for solitude. Nevertheless, for a few hours each week, in that small, windowless classroom of the group session, I was no longer alone.

About the Author

AW Schade is a Marine and Vietnam veteran with a successful post-military career as a corporate executive. Schade succumbed to PTSD in 2004 and had to take early retirement to find answers, and assistance to fight PTSD. To help other veterans he wrote his two personal stories; "The demons of war are persistent," and "Note Alone," which are both freely distributed.

For more information, please visit his website www.awschade.com where copies of the author's complete works [*Looking for God within the Kingdom or Religious Confusion; If I fail, what doom awaits the children, and more*] may be purchased. Also at Amazon, Audible, B&N etc. For media inquiries and interview requests, please contact Art Schade directly at awschade@gmail.com.

Semper Fii

‒

VA & other support groups follow
[Some links may have changed]

PTSD Resources USA

Veterans Administration (VA) www.va.gov
Vet Center www.vetcenter.va.gov
VA National Center for PTSD (Excellent Resources and Info)
www.ptsd.va.gov/

VETERAN ORGANIZATIONS

Veterans of Foreign www.vfw.org
American Legion www.legion.org
AMVETS www.amvets.org
Disabled American Veterans (DAV) www.dav.org
Iraq Afghanistan Veterans of America (IAVA) www.iava.org
Iraq War Veterans Organization (IWVO) www.iraqwarveterans.org
Marine Corps League www.mcleague.org
Military Order of the Purple Heart www.purpleheart.org
Paralyzed Veterans of America (PVA) www.pva.org
Veterans of Foreign Wars (VFW) www.vfw.org
Veterans of Modern Warfare www.modernveterans.com
Women Veterans of America www.womenveteransofamerica.com

PEER GROUPS

Vets4Vets http://www.vets4vets.us

Coalition for Iraq and Afghanistan Veterans
www.coalitionforveterans.org
America Supports You www.americasupportsyou.mil
Black Military World www.blackmilitaryworld.com
Journal of Military Experience www.militaryexperience.org
Coming Home Project www.cominghomeproject.net
Give an Hour www.giveanhour.org
Grace After Fire www.graceafterfire.org
Helmets to Hardhats www.helmetstohardhats.org
Hire Heroes USA www.hireheroesusa.org
Marine Parents www.marineparents.com
Military.com www.military.com

Military One Source www.militaryonesource.com
National Veterans Foundation www.nvf.org
Operation Homefront Operation Vets www.operationvets.org
Patriot Guard Riders www.patriotguard.org
Soldiers Angels www.soldiersangels.org
Swords-to-Plowshares www.swords-to-plowshares.org
T.A.P.S www.taps.org
United We Serve www.unitedweservemil.org
Michele Rosenthal, HEAL MY PTSD, LLC www.healmyptsd.com
Wounded Warrior Project www.woundedwarriorproject.org
Salem-News Newsroom <newsroom@salem-news.com>
VETSROCK http://www.vetsrock.org Veteran charity to provide basic
needs such as food and shelter to as many veterans in need as we can.
Military Order of the Purple Heart Service Foundation –
http://www.mophsf.org
Veterans Vocational Technical Institute – http://www.vvti.org/

In addition to PTSD, Veterans should be aware of help they can receive for Mesothelioma
Cancer at: http://www.mesotheliomasymptoms.com/ Mesothelioma is a
very deadly form of cancer made up of four main types, which impact 2,000 to 3,000
Americans every year. The first form of this disease is pleural mesothelioma, which
develops in the lining of the lungs. This cancer of the lungs can cause many serious side-
effects, including hoarseness, shortness of breath, fluid buildup in the lungs, sharp chest
pains, coughing up blood, a loss of muscle function, and extreme swelling. Pleural
mesothelioma makes up for the highest percentage of mesothelioma cases.

Printed in Great Britain
by Amazon